LIJIANG

丽　江

FOREIGN LANGUAGES PRESS　BEIJING
外文出版社　北京

LIJIANG

A mountain formation movement, which took place 65 million years ago and which created the Himalayas, known as the "roof of the world," gave rise to the Qinghai-Tibet Plateau. In the southeastern part of this plateau and the northwestern part of the Yunnan-Guizhou Plateau, meandering mountain ranges tower to the sky and swift rivers roar in deep gorges, presenting magnificent landforms over an area covering more than 200,000 sq. km. This area is the beautiful Lijiang Prefecture.

The general topographical features of Lijiang Prefecture are characterized by highland in the northwest and lowland in the southeast, with a very sharp fall in altitude. The prefecture is mainly composed of the Jinsha River canyon area and a number of huge mountain chains. The entire prefecture can be taken as a topographical wonder encompassing hilly lands, big and small rivers, lakes and pools, gaping valleys, and narrow and precipitous gorges.

The prefecture boasts over 90 rivers and streams, which mainly belong to the two systems of the Jinsha and Lancang rivers. In addition, there are numerous natural lakes formed from extremely limpid glacier water. These lakes are completely free of pollution.

Its unique geographical location, together with its rivers and mountains, endows Lijiang Prefecture with a varied climate, rich vegetation cover and abundant forest resources. Its plants include those native to tropical, temperate and frigid zones. The thick forest and good vegetation cover provide an ideal habitat for a large variety of wild animals, among which is the famous Yunnan snub-nosed monkey.

There are many tourist attractions in Lijiang Prefecture. For instance, the 13 snow-covered peaks of the Yulong (Jade Dragon) Mountains, with their main peak towering 5,596 meters above sea level, stretch for over 30 kilometers in an unbroken chain. Facing the Yulong Mountains across the Jinsha River are the snow-covered Haba Mountains. The roaring current of the Jinsha River races past between the two mountain ranges. On the river is the famous Hutiao (Leaping Tiger) Gorge. The altitude difference between the bottom of the gorge and the top of the highest peak exceeds 3,000 m. The scenery in the Yulong Mountains can be taken as the epitome of the natural landscapes in Lijiang. It comprises glaciers, thick snowfields, waterfalls, primeval forests, precipitous peaks and grassy marshlands. Apart from the Yulong Mountains, there are such tourist wonders as the Jiushijiu (Ninety-Nine) Dragon Pool, which lies on the Laojun (Old-Man) Mountain like a piece of green jade. This highland lake came into being as a result of erosion by ice, and the rich vegetation around it is a wondrous sight all the year round. Around Lugu Lake, which looks like a shining sapphire hidden deep in the mountains, live the matriarchal Mosuo people. Chenghai and Lingyuanqing lakes in Yongsheng County are other tourist attractions, as is the gigantic "V" bend in the Yangtze River, and the Baoshan Rock City, built on a mushroom-shaped gigantic rock and linked with the outside world by only one narrow trail.

Lijiang Prefecture is home to people of more than 20 minority ethnic groups, the bulk of whom are the Naxi. Each of these ethnic groups has a unique culture and history, which match into the beauty of the land, setting an example of a harmonious relationship between man and nature.

The Naxi ethnic group has a long history, and its origin can be traced back to the ancient nomadic Diqiang tribe. The majority of the Naxi have settled in the northwestern part of Yunnan as a compact community after long years of migration. Now, the Naxi population in Lijiang exceeds 200,000. In both the ancient cities and scattered villages, people can still witness traces of the unique Naxi historical culture and folk customs. The most typical examples are the Dongba ("necromancer" or "sutra reader") culture and ancient Naxi music. The rich Dongba culture includes pictographic records, drawings on different sorts of materials, music, dance, sacrificial rituals and folk customs. Created more than 1,000 years ago, the Naxi pictographs are still used today. For instance, more than 20,000 volumes of the Dongba Sutra are written with such pictographs. The sutra is regarded as an encyclopedia for the study of the culture of the Naxi ethnic group.

In their long history of social and historical development, the Naxi people have developed the tradition of worshipping nature, gods and ghosts, thus giving rise to a great number of shamans in charge of various sacrificial and religious rituals. These rituals are characterized by the performance of ancient dances peculiar to the Dongba culture.

The Naxi people are good at studying and assimilating the cultural achievements of other ethnic groups. One example is Naxi music. It represents a crystallization of their cultural exchanges with other ethnic groups. Called the Dongjing (Cave Sutra) music of Lijiang, it is a combination of the quintessence of the ancient Naxi music with the Confucian and Daoist musical traditions of the Han people. It is considered a "living fossil of the ancient music of China."

The cultural phenomena of the Naxi ethnic group appear to be very complicated. Yet, the core of their culture reflects the experience of the ancient Naxi people, who underwent all the hardships of migration and came to revere the power of nature. They developed a rare ability to reach harmony with the natural environment—the mountains and the rivers. This cultural heritage has survived and can be witnessed in the daily life of the Naxi people in Lijiang Prefecture today.

The ancient city of Lijiang is located at the foot of the snow-capped Yulong Mountains. Known as the "soul of Lijiang," the city forms a part of the cultural heritage of both China and the world as a whole.

The ancient city of Lijiang, which has been included in the United Nations' "World Cultural Heritage" list, is in fact formed of three separate ancient towns, namely, Baisha, Shuhe and Dayan. It is called the "soul of Lijiang" because the city itself is located where the Han, Tibetan, Nanzhao and Naxi cultures converge and has been a caretaker of civilization for over 1,000 years. The city's cultural relics are evidence of the harmony human beings have achieved with nature and are a base for dialogue between mankind and nature in the future.

With mountains towering to sky to its northwest, the city is open to the southeast. Thus, it is sheltered from the cold winds in autumn and winter, and enjoys sunshine all the year round. Lijiang's houses are built with carved bricks and upturned eaves and are laid out in an orderly pattern. Some of them have screen walls in front. The city's undulating streets and lanes, tranquil stone-paved roads, gurgling streams flowing through houses and around courtyard walls, and stone and wooden bridges that link the lanes and courtyards all indicate the intimate and harmonious relationship the city has established with Mother Earth. The trees and flowers everywhere, the antique furniture and paintings in the age-old houses of the common folk, the sound of ancient music coming from the quiet, deep lanes all add to the unique and lingering charm of this ancient city.

The people of Lijiang live tranquil lives, and are very caring toward each other. The city is notable for its *dapinhuo*, or mutual help, activities to help the aged.

The ancient city of Lijiang is by no means a fossil. It is alive and full of vigor. Its "poetic style of living," its aesthetic norms and its simple way of life, all of which are derived from the age-old traditions which its people preserve are a treasure that has disappeared in modern cities and is hard to recover. This is perhaps the very reason why the United Nations included it in its "World Cultural Heritage" list.

The unique and gorgeous beauty of Lijiang invariably gives people an intimate feeling. It is an ideal place to visit for people who love nature and are fascinated by quaint folk customs.

丽　江

6500万年前，大陆板块的碰撞、造山运动，抬升起了世界屋脊青藏高原，在其东南边缘和今云贵高原西北部，面积20多万平方公里的土地上，云岭逶迤、江河纵流的雄奇地貌颇为壮观。这里，就是美丽的丽江。丽江地形的总趋势为西北高、东南低，海拔悬殊大。它以金沙江峡谷及山地高原为主，其间高山峡谷并列，谷坝镶嵌其中，丘陵、江河、湖泊、宽谷、峡谷并存，形成了错综复杂、千姿百态的地貌景观。丽江境内大小河流90多条，主要属金沙、澜沧两大水系。天然湖泊众多，由于均为雪水汇聚而更显明澈澄碧，毫无污染。此外，特殊的地理位置、山河的走势和流布，以及多样的气候类型，使丽江拥有丰富的森林资源，植被茂密，植物种类繁多，热带、温带、寒带植物均有分布。丰富的植物资源自然使众多野生动物，包括滇金丝猴等珍奇动物都能找到最适宜的安家之地，为它们的生息繁衍提供了良好环境。大自然的山水灵气，动、植物的和谐相生，构成了丽江佳景天成、美仑美奂的奇丽风光。

丽江景致多样，风格各异。玉龙雪山集冰川雪海、叠泉飞瀑、原始森林、高山草甸等诸多景致于一体，雄浑壮美，是丽江自然风光的代表；主峰海拔5596米的玉龙雪山十三座雪峰，绵亘30多公里，与哈巴雪山对峙，汹涌澎湃的金沙江奔腾于两山之间，其间的虎跳峡岭谷高差达3000米以上；如翠玉撒于老君山间的九十九龙潭均为高山冰蚀湖，四季景色绚丽，生态景观丰富；泸沽湖有如熠熠生辉的蓝宝石镶嵌在逶迤的青山之间，其独有的摩梭“女儿国”风情极具奇异色彩；永胜的程海、灵源箐，以脱俗的气质而闻名远近；“万里长江第一湾”巨大的“V”字形江面显示了造化之功鞭策长江东去的豪情气概；而建在金沙江畔一整块蘑菇状巨形天然岩石上的宝山石城，只有一条路通往外界，险要而神秘。

丽江生活着以纳西族为主的二十多个少数民族，每个民族都拥有自己悠长的历史，与生养他们的这片美丽土地相辉映、相融合，休戚与共，体现出一种近乎完美的自然同凡人的契合与融洽。纳西族历史悠久，渊源于中国古代游牧民族氐羌，经历了漫长的迁徙过程，最终大部分聚居在滇西北地区，其中丽江的纳西族人口超过了20万。整个丽江，包括古城乃至众多广布的纳西乡村至今还存活着以东巴文化、纳西古乐为代表的独特历史文化遗存和民风民俗。东巴文化的蕴涵十分广博深奥，它包括象形文字、图画、经典、音乐、文学、舞蹈、仪式仪规，以及贯穿东巴教义的各种民风民俗。一千多年前纳西族创制的象形文字流传至今，用它书写的约2万多卷的《东巴经》成为纳西族的百科全书，是活着的古文字资料。在长期的社会历史发展过程中，纳西族形成了内容广泛的自然崇拜和对鬼魂、神灵的崇拜，众多特定的祭祀仪式仪规和从事宗教活动的巫师也由此产生。东巴舞蹈既保留了浓郁的原始气息，又讲究规范，艺术构思与舞蹈造型奇特。纳西族善于学习和吸收其他民族的文化成果，纳西古乐就是他们与各民族文化交流的结晶，结合纳西古代音乐的精髓、融汇汉族儒家乐与道教经腔而成的丽江洞经音乐，成为“中国古典音乐的活化石”。纳西族的种种文化现象看似庞杂，但若将其内在的本质抽出，结论必然是：曾历经风雨迁徙路的纳西族崇尚的唯有自然，他们与山、与水、与所有自然造化达成亲和的能力是千百年来思想锻造的结果，在与这种能力的互动、衍生中，终于成就了如此耐人寻味、积淀深厚的纳西文化，同时其深邃的精神内涵也随之溶入了纳西人的血液当中。所幸的是，这个人文遗产的一部分已经被物化或精神化，并已成为丽江纳西人日常生活中的重要组成部分。在丽江之魂——玉龙雪山俯瞰下的丽江古城中，这一点体现得尤为突出。丽江古城是中国古代文明和世界古代文明的遗产，具体而微则是以纳西文化为代表的民族文化结晶。

已被列入联合国“世界文化遗产名录”的丽江古城是由白沙古镇－束河古镇－大研古镇三个相对独立的城建单元共同组成的统一体。之所以称其为丽江之魂，因为古城本身就是汉、藏、古代南诏、纳西文化的交汇地，是人类上千年文明的一个载体。古城的幸存，仿佛就是古人留存下来的一篇篇旧事的注脚，是今人与造物主默契相偕的产物，是后人同未来对话的依靠。在当今钢筋、混凝土流行的水泥世界中，这座土木结构、手工建造与雕刻的城镇是如此的典雅、柔和、亲切和令人感动。它科学的选址——座靠西北，放眼东南，既可避开寒风、永浴阳光，又同玉龙雪山遥相对望，构成和谐美景；它错落有致而又通畅无阻的布局、雕砖覆瓦飞檐照壁的商肆民居，无不体现出一种艺术的规范与灵动；它起伏的街巷、清幽的石板路、过屋绕墙的汩汩流水、连巷跨院的石桥和木桥，使这座淙淙作响的城镇与大地有种难得的肌肤相亲；它怀抱下的草木花朵与古宅中的书画长案、曲径通幽处飘来的古乐清音，无不散发出古城风情画卷的独特韵味。古城的城建艺术是精典的，而古城的气息又是平和的、悠然的，时常可见的老人们的"打拼伙"活动就充分展现了古城主人和睦、互助的生活观念。丽江古城是一座现代人与之相碰触、相交流后便永难忘掉的地方，因为它绝非一座古城的标本或空壳，而是时刻洋溢着淳朴生活气息、时刻令人感觉到脉动的活着的古城。它固守的在传统中获得的"诗意的栖居"方式、美学风尚和与此相依的日常生活，正是现代城市已经丢失、并再难找回的宝贵财富。或许这也正是"世界文化遗产"里面最为珍贵、最需保留和发掘的文化内涵之一。

面对丽江美景，很多人心中自然而然便会升腾起一种亲近感和归属感，滋生出一种难以名状的情愫——在被美景包裹的同时，心也在包融和体会着深谷幽兰般的丽江。丽江是天生丽质的，又是风格独特的，它毫不哗众取宠的、绚丽而朴实的美，足以让热爱大自然、崇尚多姿多彩民族风俗的人们思考很多东西。

丽江旅游略图
TOURIST MAP OF LIJIANG
泸沽湖
Lugu Lake
奉科
Fengke
原始森林
Primeval Forest
宝山石头城
Rock Town inBaoshan
宝山
Baoshan
塔城
Tacheng
上江
Shangjiang
金沙江 Jinshajiang River
巨甸
Judian
鲁甸
Ludian
Hutiao Gorge 虎跳峡
大具
Daju
迪 庆 州
Diqing Autonomous Prefecture
黑水
Heishui
白水
Baishui
大东
Dadong
金庄
Jinzhuang
金江
Jinjiang
龙蟠
Longpan
玉龙雪山
Yulong
Snowy Mountain
黎明
Liming
黎光
Liguang
丽江植物园
Botanical Garden in Lijiang
玉峰寺
Yufeng Temple
白沙
Baisha
长江第一湾
The First Bend of Yangtze River
丽江大研镇
Dayan Town
金山
Jinshan
仁河
Renhe
石鼓镇
Shigu Town
拉市
Lashi
黄山
Huangshan
石头
Shitou
文峰寺
Wenfeng Temple
七河
Qihe
怒 江 州
Nujiang Autonomous
Prefecture
九河
Jiuhe
太安
Tai'an
九十九龙潭
Jiushijiu Dragon Pools
共河
Gonghe
老君山
Laojun Mountain
大 理 州
Dali Autonomous Prefecture

Ancient Dayan Town in Lijiang

The construction of the town started in the Song Dynasty (960-1279) and by the Ming Dynasty (1368-1644) it was already quite prosperous. The layout of the town conforms to scientific norms and forms a harmonious unity with its surrounding environment. All the ordinary houses are wood-brick structures, extremely elegant and comfortable.

丽江大研古镇

始建于宋代，明代已呈繁荣景象，“瓦房栉比”，“环市列肆”。古城不筑城墙，以高山为墙，深谷为地。古城四周青山、玉水萦回，建筑布局合理，与自然景观和谐辉映。民居均为土木结构，舒适优美，至今依旧维持古貌。

Yulong Mountains
Consisting of 13 snow-covered peaks, this mountain range stretches for 35 km. The highest peak, "Shanzidou," is 5,596 m. above sea level. On the mountain is a glacier, which is the southernmost of its kind in the Northern Hemisphere. Halfway up the range are large tracts of primeval forest and grassy marshland.

玉龙雪山
由 13 座连绵雪峰组成,纵长 35 公里,主峰扇子陡海拔 5596 米,分布着北半球最南端的现代冰川。山腰至山脚为大片原始森林及草甸所覆盖,集壮观和秀美于一体。

◁ **Yuquan (Jade Spring) Park**
Located at the foot of Xiangshan (Elephant) Hill to the north of Lijiang City, the park is built around Yuquan Lake (also called "Black Dragon Pool"). The crystal-clear water in the lake comes from underground springs. Amid the green trees in the park are many Naxi-style structures built in the Ming and Qing (1644-1911) dynasties, such as the Deyue Tower and Yiwen Pavilion. Of these, the most attractive is probably the Wufeng Tower.

玉泉公园
位于丽江城北象山脚下,又称黑龙潭,汇集地下涌泉而成。湖水清澈,古木葱郁。园内有明清两代众多的纳西族建筑,如得月楼、一文亭等,其中以五凤楼最富特色。

A view of the Yulong Mountains in early morning.
玉龙雪山晨景

16

The Baishui (White Water) River.
白水河

Ganhaizi, at the foot of the Yulong Mountains, is an area of natural grassy marshland formed when a highland lake dried up. The local people say it was still water-logged in the 1940s. Now, it is an ideal place to watch the sun rising from behind the glacier and the moon going down behind the snow-covered peaks.

玉龙山下的甘海子。是由一个高山湖泊干涸而形成的天然草甸,四十年代还是一个冰渍湖。这里可观赏日出冰川、月下雪峰。

Yunshanping is a grassy marshland situated amid old and fantastically shaped dragon spruce (Picea asperata) trees. With the Yulong Mountains in the background, it is green in spring and summer, and white in autumn and winter. In a Naxi legend it is called the "Third State of the Jade Dragon" and the "Garden of Eternal Love."

云杉坪,一块被古老的茂密云杉林环绕的大草甸,这里有玉龙雪山做背景,春夏绿草如茵,秋冬银装素裹。是纳西族传说中的"玉龙第三国"、"爱情伊甸园"。

The Wufeng (Five-phoenix) Tower ▷

The tower was built in the 29th year of the Wanli reign period of the Ming Dynasty (1601). It is a three-storied building and the upturned eaves of each story have eight angles. From any place within the tower, one can see the colorful images of five flying phoenixes.

五凤楼

始建于明万历 29 年(1601 年),楼呈"亚"字形,楼台三叠,屋檐八角,共 24 个飞檐,任何角度都能见其似 5 只彩凤展翅飞舞。

The Wangu (Eternal) Tower

A monumental building located in the ancient city of Lijiang, the tower is an example of wooden *dougong* architecture (with sets of brackets on top of the columns supporting the beams within and the roof eaves without. A set that is cushioned with trapezoidal blocks is called *dou*, and one that consists of tiers of outstretching arms is called *gong*). Thirty-three m. high, the tower has five stories and five tiers of eaves. The top story has 13 angles, representing the 13 peaks of the Yulong Mountains. Painted inside the tower are 2,300 auspicious patterns, representing the harmony and unity of the 23 ethnic groups living in Lijiang. The colorful murals in the tower are redolent of the traditional Dongba culture of the Naxi people.

万古楼

丽江古城的标志性建筑，楼阁式五层五重檐全木结构斗拱建筑，高 33 米，屋顶 13 个角代表玉龙十三峰，2300 个吉祥图案代表丽江 23 个民族和睦相处。楼内的彩绘和壁画具有浓厚的纳西东巴文化和传统文化色彩。

The large stone bridge in Dayan Town

According to historical records, the bridge was already in existence when the imperial troops of the Yuan Dynasty entered Lijiang in 1253. At that time, the area around the bridge served as an army camp and drilling ground.

大研镇中大石桥

据史料记载,1253 年元军进入丽江时已存在,当时其周围为元军驻扎和操练地。

A typical small bridge across a stream

Numerous limpid streams, arising from Black Dragon Pool, crisscross Lijiang City, dividing it into several sections, which are again linked up by many plain wooden bridges and buildings across these streams, making it a "city upon the water."

小桥流水

丽江古城的水源自黑龙潭，水质清冽，环城绕院，形成主街傍河、小巷临水、跨水筑楼的景象，而一座座古朴木桥又将被分割的区域连成一个整体，构成了独特的水城风韵。

The Baima Longtan Triple Wells

In the ancient city of Lijiang there are many artesian wells grouped in threes. The local people make different uses of these wells according to the direction of the water flow: The one furthest upstream is used for drinking water, the middle one is used to wash vegetables, and the one furthest downstream to wash clothes.

白马龙潭三眼井

丽江古城中有多处三眼井,水井相邻,井水自然流出。人们自觉遵循民间传统,顺水流方向使用:上眼井饮水,中眼井洗菜,下眼井洗衣。

Clear water running through the kitchen of a Naxi family
When the stream originating in the Yuquan reaches Dayan Town, it first divides into three, and then into numerous small streamlets. These streamlets flow either in front or at the back of the houses of hundreds of families. For better convenience, many families even lead the water into their houses and kitchens.

水流入户
清水从这户纳西人家的厨房下流过。玉泉水流至大研城头便岔开三路，再分成无数小支流，蜿蜒穿过千家万户的门前屋后，许多家引水入院，用水极为便利。

In Lijiang, many springs produce potable water. This spring is called “Canyi.”

古城中许多地方都有泉水可供饮用。这处泉眼称作“璨溢”。

A view of Sifang Street in Lijiang ▷

Originally a square developed on the basis of a former country market, Sifang Street is now the center for business and other activities in Lijiang. Lined with shops on all sides, it bustles with activity all day long.

古城四方街一角

四方街是由村落露天集市演化而成的商业广场,小街道从四个方向辐射延伸开去。它是古城的活动和商贸中心,四周店铺林立,熙攘热闹。

Morning in Lijiang.

古城的早晨

A part of the ancient city of Lijiang.
古城一隅

A street in Lijiang.
古城一条街

Top: A handicraft store in Dayan Town. **Middle**: Elderly Naxi women hawking home-made handicraft articles that display strong ethnic characteristics. **Bottom**: In Lijiang, elderly folks are good at making local snacks. Jelly made with *Jidou* (chicken bean) starch, as shown here, is much favored by tourists.

上图:大研镇工艺品商店。中图:心灵手巧的纳西老人出售自己缝制的民族工艺品。下图:丽江许多老人都会做纳西风味小吃,图中这种鸡豆凉粉很受欢迎。

In Lijiang, ordinary houses are built in different styles

For instance, there is the type called "one gate and two courtyards" and the type called "houses on three sides and screen wall on the other." The type shown in the picture is called "four abodes with five courtyards." Most of the houses are two-storied and have spacious courtyards paved with stone slabs and dotted with trees and flowers.

纳西族民居

古城中民居的形式很多,有的是"一进两院",有的是"三坊一照壁"。此形式的院落也称"四合五天井"式,房多为双层,院落宽敞,以石间隔铺地,以花木装点。

Daintily designed traditional houses in Lijiang ▷

In this courtyard, cobblestones are used to compose a symbolic pattern of longevity with the images of four bats.

设计讲究的古城民居

这个院中用石子拼成的图案称"四蝠圆寿"。

Eave tiles on the roof of an old building in Lijiang.
古城建筑屋顶上的瓦当。

In Lijiang, a lot of wine shops and inns nestle in traditional courtyards.

古城里许多酒店、客栈都座落在这样大大小小的传统院落中。

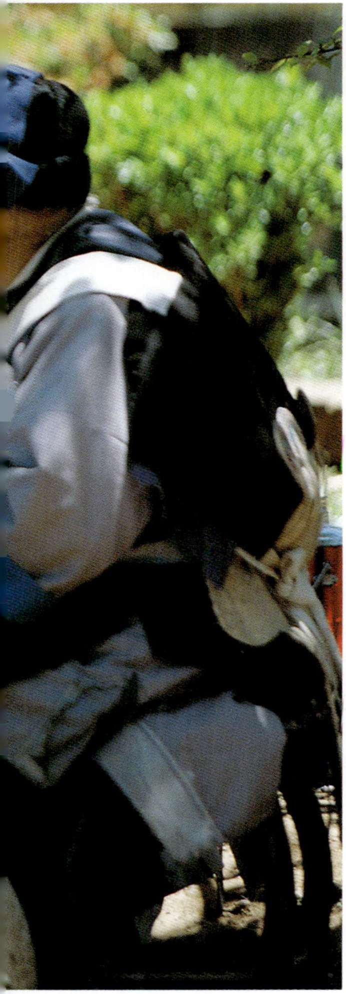

Old folks playing cards

Among the elderly people in Lijiang there is a long-established mutual-help tradition called *Huacong* or *dapinhuo*. It is said that this tradition has a history of several hundred years. The custom is for each of the elderly people in a neighborhood to lay aside a certain amount of money from his or her income each month and give it to one designated elderly person. This person will use the money to hold several collective activities in the month. Most of these activities are recreational in nature, including hosting dinners, tea parties and card or mahjong games. In the past, the purpose of pooling money was to help those in difficulty. Now, it has evolved into a recreational fund for the old folks. Most of the old women have grown up together. Their average age is 80.

玩纸牌的丽江老人

这里的老人有种传统的民间互助活动叫"化琮"或叫"打拼伙",据说已有数百年的历史。他(她)们每人每月拿出数十元或上百元钱交给一个人集中使用并轮流做东,每月组织几次活动,在一起吃饭、喝茶、闲谈、玩纸牌或麻将消遣。过去以集资互助帮人为目的,如今已成为一种民间娱乐方式。这些老人,她们从小一起长大,如今平均年龄已近八十岁。

Site where sacrifices are made to heaven according to the rites of the Dongba religion. The sacrificial rites are in a sense a showcase of the themes of the Dongba religion and Naxi culture as a whole.

东巴祭祀活动中的祭天道场，进行的祭祀仪式立体展现了纳西族宗教信仰和文化追求的一个主题。

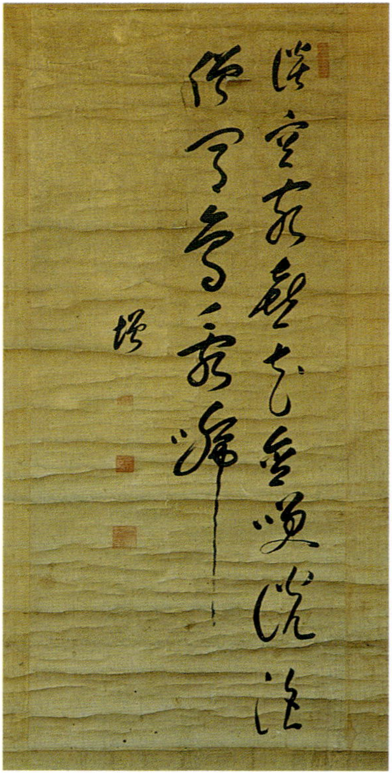

A couplet written in cursive calligraphy by Mu Zeng over 300 years ago

Mu Zeng was an outstanding Naxi tribal chieftain in the Ming Dynasty. He made great contributions to the governing of Lijiang. Mu Zeng was well versed in the Han and Tibetan cultures, and wrote several books of poems. Together with a senior Buddhist monk in Tibet, he presided over the printing of the 108-volume bKa-gyur (Collection of Tibetan Buddhist Scriptures).

木增手书，一幅距今已 300 多年的草书对联

木增曾是明代一位对丽江治理有方的土司，他崇尚汉藏文化，著有数卷诗集，并与一西藏活佛一起主持刊印丽江版《甘珠尔》108 卷。

He Xuewen is a veteran Dongba. In the Naxi language, "Dongba" means "necromancer" or "scripture reader." They are the principal propagators of Dongba culture.

老东巴和学文。"东巴"是东巴教中的祭司，意为占卜者或诵经者，是东巴文化主要的继承者和传播人。

A hand-written copy of a Dongba classic.
纳西族东巴文的民间手抄本。

Dongba painting
The most representative artistic legacy of the ancient pictorial art of the Naxi ethnic group includes timber slat painting, paperboard painting, bamboo painting and scroll paintings of images of celestial beings.

东巴画
纳西古画中一种最原始、最有代表性的艺术遗产。主要有木牌画、竹笔画、纸牌画、神轴画等。

Part of the painting *Divine Road*, a long hand-scroll of Dongba painting
The scroll is about 15 meters long and more than 30 centimeters wide. Unconventionally conceived and brightly colored, the images in the painting are extremely vivid, showing the natural beauty of the local primitive art.

东巴画长卷"神路图"局部
图卷长约 15 米，宽 30 多厘米，构思别致、色彩鲜艳、形象生动，呈现出一种原始艺术的自然美。其内容由十八层地狱到人类世界，再到天国，描绘了众多人物及鬼怪，场面宏大，具有极高的艺术和历史价值。

In the Naxi language, timber slat painting is called *kebiao*. The slat is usually made of pine. It is about 33 cm. long and has a sharpened end at the bottom to make it easy to insert somewhere. On the slats are depicted ghosts and other celestial beings. A unique Naxi art form, the paintings are used in sacrificial ceremonies.

东巴木牌画。纳西语称"课标"，一般由松木制作，长约尺余，下端削尖以便竖插。上绘各种鬼怪妖魔或自然神类，形态古朴，主要用于东巴祭祀活动，是纳西族独有的民族艺术形式。

Ancient Naxi music
Most of the players of these instruments are elderly veteran Naxis. The music they play is based on the music of the Tang and Song dynasties.

纳西古乐
这支民间音乐社团的演奏者大多是年逾古稀的纳西族老人，他们以唐宋音乐为原型的古乐演奏令人陶醉。

Naxi elders performing "Baisha Xiyue" (Baisha Fine Music)
This music is unique to Naxi people living in Lijiang. It is a complete series of ritual music specially composed to pacify the souls of those died in war. The performance is sometimes enlivened with singing and holds a great emotional appeal.

白沙村演奏白沙细乐的纳西族老人
白沙细乐为纳西语"崩时司礼"的意释，意为超度巴人亡灵的安魂礼乐，产生于元代初期，是一部完整表现一次部落战争的大型音乐套曲。乐曲以器乐演奏为主，间有轻歌吟唱，情调高雅、意境深远。

Houses of ordinary people in the ancient town of Baisha

Baisha Town was once the political, economic and cultural center for the areas inhabited mainly by the Naxi people in Lijiang. In the center of the town one can still see quite a number of monastery buildings as well as a large square that was the seat of political power in the past. To the west of the square is a long, narrow area for business and cultural activities.

白沙古镇民居

白沙镇曾是前丽江及纳西族地区的政治、经济文化中心。镇中心有被称为"木都"的殿宇群落和象征政治权力的大广场，其西是一个窄长的商业文化广场。

The wooden gate tower of Baisha Village is in typical Naxi architectural style, reminiscent of architecture of the Ming Dynasty.

纳西建筑白沙木门楼。它保留了明代建筑的风格。

The Baisha murals, titled *Sakyamuni Explaining the Scriptures*, focus on the dissemination of Buddhism in both inland China and Tibet. They also depict some Taoist stories. The murals contain more than 100 human figures. They are rare pieces of art because they embody the traditions of two religions and give expression to the painting techniques and styles of several ethnic groups at the same time.

著名的白沙壁画——《如来讲经传教图》。壁画展示了藏传佛教、汉传佛教、道教等宗教活动和故事，画面中有大小100多个人物画像，线条精细，色彩艳丽，突出特点是多种宗教内容合一，多民族传统绘画技巧与风格交融，可以说是稀世奇珍。

The famous Baisha murals and the interior of the Dabaoji Palace

The Dabaoji Palace, which was built in the Ming Dynasty, comprises three courtyards surrounded by spacious buildings of thick and solid *dougong* structure. In the palace there are more than 20 ancient murals.

白沙壁画和大宝积宫内景

大宝积宫建于明代，三进院落，柱梁粗实，斗拱雄健，宽敞壮观，内有壁画二十余幅。

***Jidou* bean trellis in Shuhe Village**
Jidou (chicken bean) is a kind of bean that is only produced in Lijiang, and is the main ingredient in bean jelly.

束河村里的"鸡豆架"
"鸡豆"是丽江特有的一种做凉粉的豆子。

◁ **The ancient town of Shuhe**
Shuhe is famous for its production of leather goods, and bronze and silver ware. The products are much sought after in Tibet, the areas inhabited by Tibetans in Yunnan and Sichuan, and India.

束河古镇
是丽江最有特色的商业集镇之一,以皮革制品和铜器、银器生产著称。其产品在印度、中国西藏及康巴藏区享有盛誉。

Shigu (Stone Drum) Town at twilight
Located at the bottom end of the "V" bend on the Yangtze River, Shigu Town boasts a long history and beautiful scenery.

暮色下的石鼓镇
石鼓镇建在长江第一湾湾底，历史悠久，景色秀丽。

Stone drum
Standing in a pavilion in Shigu Town, this drum-shaped stone tablet is 75-cm. thick and 150 cm. in diameter. Local legend has it that it was erected by Zhuge Liang, a famous strategist in the Three Kingdoms Period (220-280). The epigraph carved on the tablet is of great historical value.

石鼓
厚 75 厘米、直径 150 厘米的巨大鼓状石碣，立于石鼓镇中一座亭子里。传说为三国时期(220－280 年)军事家诸葛亮所立，上刻明代丽江土司征战的纪功诗文，极有历史价值。

Tiehong Bridge by Shigu Town
Some 17 m. long, the bridge was built in 1888 with thick iron chains and wooden planks. It is used to be a strategic point on the ancient "South Silk Road" and Yunnan-Tibet road for tea transport.

石鼓镇边铁虹桥
始建于 1888 年，长 17 米，以铁链做梁，铺以木板，至今仍在使用。是中国古代南丝绸之路和滇藏"茶马古道"的要津。

The "V" bend on the Yangtze River
Upon reaching Shigu Town, the Yangtze River suddenly forms a "V" bend. On both sides of the river, green willow trees grow luxuriously over large tracts of fertile land.

长江第一湾
海拔 1850 米，中国第一大河在丽江石鼓镇突然一个"V"字调头，江面宽阔，气势壮观，两岸青柳成行，良田广布。

Hutiao (Leaping Tiger) Gorge

The Jinsha River roars between the Haba Mountains and the Yulong Mountains, bringing into being the famous Hutiao Gorge. In the narrowest part, the river is only some 20-m. wide, and in the water there are several reefs. It is said that once a tiger jumped from reef to reef in order to across the gorge.

虎跳峡

金沙江在哈巴和玉龙两山中间咆哮而过,形成举世闻名的虎跳峡。它全长 17 公里,江面最窄处仅 20 余米。江心有数处礁石,相传老虎曾借石跃过峡谷,故得名虎跳峡。

Old camellia in Yufeng Monastery

Built in the 39th year of the Kangxi reign period (1700) of the Qing Dynasty, the monastery is the largest of the 13 in Lijiang. In the monastery is a camellia tree, which is 500 years old. The tree is in bloom from early spring to mid-summer. Notable is the fact that the different branches of the tree bloom at different periods, producing altogether over 10, 000 flowers a year. It is one of Lijiang's scenic wonders.

玉峰寺中的万朵茶花树

玉峰寺是丽江十三大喇嘛寺中规模最大的一个，建于清康熙 39 年(1700 年)，藏名特拉西卓飞林。寺中有一棵茶花树，树龄约 500 年，每年茶花分 20 多批立春初放，立夏花尽，每批千余朵。开放时繁花似锦，成为丽江一大景观。

Zhiyun Monastery
Another of the 13 monasteries, it was first built in the fifth year of the Yongzheng reign period (1727) of the Qing Dynasty and expanded in the fifth year of the Guangxu reign period (1879) of the same dynasty. ***Bottom***: Murals are still visible in the ruins of Zhiyun Monastery.

指云寺
藏名吉东峰卓林，清雍正 5 年(1727 年)始建，光绪 5 年(1879 年)续建。相传寺前拉市海落水洞中，保留有莲花祖师的足迹。为丽江十三大寺之一。下图为指云寺遗址彩绘。

Baoshan Rock City
Dating from the Yuan Dynasty (1271-1368), the village perches on a huge mushroom-shaped rock. There is only one road connecting it with the outside world. Over 90 Naxi families live in the village, all using tools and utensils made of natural rock.

宝山石城
元代时建造,建在一块独立的蘑菇状巨形岩石上,十分险要,只有一条路通往外界。城中有九十余户纳西族人家居住,所用器具均为天然岩石凿制,堪称奇绝。

Marlboro

Terraced fields on mountain slopes beneath Baoshan Rock City.
石城下的梯田

The only pathway in the rock city.
宝山石城内唯一一条道路。

Danxia topography at Dawn

"Danxia" is a term derived from Mount Danxia in Guangdong Province. It is used to refer to topography mainly formed by red sandstone. This area covers more than 200 sq. km., making it the largest piece of Danxia land in China. Here, grotesque rocks and mountain peaks form a surreal red landscape.

黎明的丹霞地貌

"丹霞"之名源自中国广东省丹霞山,用以指红砂岩为主的地貌。黎明丹霞地貌面积200多平方公里,是中国最大的丹霞地貌区。

61

View of the area around Zimei Pool on Laojun Mountain.

老君山姊妹潭风光

63

Viewing the Yulong Mountains from Laojun Mountain.
自老君山远眺玉龙雪山。

The scenery of Laojun Mountain

Located in the middle of the scenic area of northern Yunnan, where three major rivers run parallel, Laojun Mountain offers numerous tourist attractions, including an azalea forest and the Jiushijiu (Ninety-Nine) Dragon Pool. In addition, the mountain boasts rich fauna and flora resources.

老君山风光

老君山地处滇西北三江并流风景区的中部，有杜鹃林、九十九龙潭、鸟王山等景点。景色绚丽多姿，动植物资源丰富。

Lugu Lake in Ninglang
Some 2,680 m. above sea level, the lake covers 50 sq. km., and the average depth of the water is 45 m. Surrounded by green hills on all sides, the lake, which is dotted with several islets, exudes an air of mysterious calm. Living around the lake are people of the Mosuo ethnic group.

宁蒗泸沽湖
海拔 2680 米，面积近 50 平方公里，平均水深 45 米，透明度达 12—14 米。为青山环抱，神秘、恬穆，湖面上点缀若干小岛，摩梭人环湖而居。

Guozhuang dance of the Mosuo people
摩梭人的锅桩舞

Men of the Yi ethnic group in the Lesser Liangshan Mountains in the northeastern part of Lijiang Prefecture.

丽江东北部小凉山的彝族汉子

The "Big Black God of Heaven" unearthed in Yongsheng.
永胜出土的"大黑天神"塑像。

Yongsheng, located in the middle part of northerm Yunnan, used to be the corridor for a massive migration of people as well as an impertant thoroughfare on the ancient "South Silk Road." The green mountains and limpid waters here offer rich matural produce. This picture shows the rural scenery in Yongsheng.

永胜地处滇西北中部，是历史上民族大迁徙的走廊，南方古丝绸之路的重要通道。这里山青水秀，物产丰富，图为永胜田园风光。

图书在版编目(CIP)数据
丽江:/洪卫东编。一北京:外文出版社,1999.3
ISBN 7-119-02343-8

Ⅰ.丽… Ⅱ.洪… Ⅲ.风光摄影-云南-丽江地区-摄影集 Ⅳ.J426.742
中国版本图书馆 CIP 数据核字(98)第 38521 号

Compiled by: Hong Weidong
Text by: Wei Aijun
Photos by: Cheng Weidong Zhao Ting Jiang Jian
Zhang Yu Xing Yi Lan Peijin
Liu Jianming Zhang Wenyin
Chen Keqin Yang Fashun
Translated by: Li Zhenguo
Edited by: Lan Peijin Wei Aijun
Designed by: Yuan Qing

First edition 1999
Second edition 2000

Lijiang

ISBN 7-119-02343-8

Published by Foreign Languages Press
24 Baiwanzhuang Road, Beijing 100037, China
Home Page: http://www.flp.com.cn
E-mail Addresses: info@flp.com.cn
sales@flp.com.cn
Printed in the People's Republic of China

编辑:洪卫东
撰文:韦爱君
摄影:成卫东 陈克勤 杨发顺 赵 汀
刘建明 张文银 蒋 剑 张 禹
邢 毅 兰佩瑾
翻译:李振国
责任编辑:兰佩瑾 韦爱君
设计:元 青

丽 江

洪卫东 编

外文出版社出版
(中国北京百万庄大街 24 号)
邮政编码 100037
外文出版社网页:http://www.flp.com.cn
外文出版社电子邮件地址:info@flp.com.cn
sales@flp.com.cn
天时印刷(深圳)有限公司印刷
1999 年(24 开)第一版
2000 年第一版第二次印刷
(英汉)
ISBN 7-119-02343-8/J·1472(外)
004800(精)